Symphony No. 6
in F Major, Op. 68
"Pastorale"

Ludwig van Beethoven

DOVER PUBLICATIONS, INC.
Mineola, New York

Published in Canada by General Publishing Company, Ltd., 30 Lesmill Road, Don Mills, Toronto, Ontario.

Published in the United Kingdom by Constable and Company, Ltd., 3 The Lanchesters, 162–164 Fulham Palace Road, London W6 9ER.

Bibliographical Note

This Dover edition, first published in 1998, is a republication of music from *Symphonies de Beethoven. Partitions d'Orchestre,* originally published by Henry Litolff's Verlag, Braunschweig, n.d.

International Standard Book Number: 0–486–40123-5

Manufactured in the United States of America
Dover Publications, Inc., 31 East 2nd Street, Mineola, N.Y. 11501

CONTENTS

*Dedicated to Prince Franz Joseph von Lobkowitz
and Count Andrey Kyrilovich Razumovsky*

Symphony No. 6
in F Major, Op. 68
("Pastorale")

(1808)

INSTRUMENTATION

Piccolo [Flauto piccolo, Fl. pic.]
2 Flutes [Flauti, Fl.]
2 Oboes [Oboi, Ob.]
2 Clarinets in Bb("B") [Clarinetti, Cl.]
2 Bassoons [Fagotti, Fag.]

2 Horns in F, Bb("B") [Corni, Cor.]
2 Trumpets in C, Eb("Es") [Trombe, Tr.]
Alto Trombone [Tb. Alto]
Tenor Trombone [Tb. Tenore]

Timpani [Tp.]

Violins I, II [Violino]
Violas [Viola]
Cellos & Basses [Violoncello (Vcl.) e Basso/i]

Symphony No. 6

in F Major, Op. 68
"Pastorale"

[I]

Erwachen heiterer Empfindungen bei der Ankunft dem Lande

Awakening of cheerful feelings on arrival in the country

1

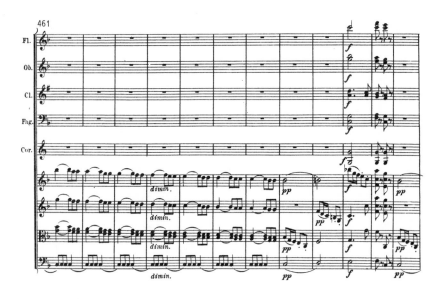

Scene am Bach
Scene by the brook

[III]
Lustiges Zusammensein in der Landleute
Merry gathering of the countryfolk

39

[IV]
Gewitter. Sturm
Thunderstorm

47

[V]
Hirtengesang. Frohe und dankbare Gefühle nach dem Sturm
Shepherd's song. Happy and grateful feelings after the storm

END OF EDITION

DOVER FULL-SIZE
ORCHESTRAL SCORES

THE SIX BRANDENBURG CONCERTOS AND THE FOUR ORCHESTRAL SUITES IN FULL SCORE, Johann Sebastian Bach. Complete standard Bach-Gesellschaft editions in large, clear format. Study score. 273pp. 9 × 12. 23376-6 Pa. **$11.95**

COMPLETE CONCERTI FOR SOLO KEYBOARD AND OR-CHESTRA IN FULL SCORE, Johann Sebastian Bach. Bach's seven complete concerti for solo keyboard and orchestra in full score from the authoritative Bach-Gesellschaft edition. 206pp. 9 × 12.
24929-8 Pa. **$11.95**

THE THREE VIOLIN CONCERTI IN FULL SCORE, Johann Sebastian Bach. Concerto in A Minor, BWV 1041; Concerto in E Major, BWV 1042; and Concerto for Two Violins in D Minor, BWV 1043. Bach-Gesellschaft edition. 64pp. 9⅜ × 12¼. 25124-1 Pa. **$6.95**

GREAT ORGAN CONCERTI, OPP. 4 & 7, IN FULL SCORE, George Frideric Handel. 12 organ concerti composed by great Baroque master are reproduced in full score from the *Deutsche Handelgesellschaft* edition. 138pp. 9⅜ × 12¼. 24462-8 Pa. **$8.95**

COMPLETE CONCERTI GROSSI IN FULL SCORE, George Frideric Handel. Monumental Opus 6 Concerti Grossi, Opus 3 and "Alexander's Feast" Concerti Grossi—19 in all—reproduced from most authoritative edition. 258pp. 9⅜ × 12¼. 24187-4 Pa. **$13.95**

LATER SYMPHONIES, Wolfgang A. Mozart. Full orchestral scores to last symphonies (Nos. 35–41) reproduced from definitive Breitkopf & Härtel Complete Works edition. Study score. 285pp. 9 × 12.
23052-X Pa. **$12.95**

PIANO CONCERTOS NOS. 17–22, Wolfgang Amadeus Mozart. Six complete piano concertos in full score, with Mozart's own cadenzas for Nos. 17–19. Breitkopf & Härtel edition. Study score. 370pp. 9⅜ × 12¼.
23599-8 Pa. **$16.95**

PIANO CONCERTOS NOS. 23–27, Wolfgang Amadeus Mozart. Mozart's last five piano concertos in full score, plus cadenzas for Nos. 23 and 27, and the Concert Rondo in D Major, K.382. Breitkopf & Härtel edition. Study score. 310pp. 9⅜ × 12¼. 23600-5 Pa. **$13.95**

THREE ORCHESTRAL WORKS IN FULL SCORE: Academic Festival Overture, Tragic Overture and Variations on a Theme by Joseph Haydn, Johannes Brahms. Reproduced from the authoritative Breitkopf & Härtel edition three of Brahms's great orchestral favorites. Editor's commentary in German and Engiish. 112pp. 9⅜ × 12¼.

24637-X Pa. **$8.95**

COMPLETE CONCERTI IN FULL SCORE, Johannes Brahms. Piano Concertos Nos. 1 and 2; Violin Concerto, Op. 77; Concerto for Violin and Cello, Op. 102. Definitive Breitkopf & Härtel edition. 352pp. 9⅜ × 12¼.

24170-X Pa. **$15.95**

COMPLETE SYMPHONIES IN FULL SCORE, Robert Schumann. No. 1 in B-flat Major, Op. 38 ("Spring"); No. 2 in C Major, Op. 61; No. 3 in E Flat Major, Op. 97 ("Rhenish"); and No. 4 in D Minor, Op. 120. Breitkopf & Härtel editions. Study score. 416pp. 9⅜ × 12¼.

24013-4 Pa. **$18.95**

GREAT WORKS FOR PIANO AND ORCHESTRA IN FULL SCORE, Robert Schumann. Collection of three superb pieces for piano and orchestra, including the popular Piano Concerto in A Minor. Breitkopf & Härtel edition. 183pp. 9⅜ × 12¼.

24340-0 Pa. **$10.95**

THE PIANO CONCERTOS IN FULL SCORE, Frédéric Chopin. The authoritative Breitkopf & Härtel full-score edition in one volume of Piano Concertos No. 1 in E Minor and No. 2 in F Minor. 176pp. 9 × 12.

25835-1 Pa. **$10.95**

THE PIANO CONCERTI IN FULL SCORE, Franz Liszt. Available in one volume the Piano Concerto No. 1 in E-flat Major and the Piano Concerto No. 2 in A Major—are among the most studied, recorded and performed of all works for piano and orchestra. 144pp. 9 × 12.

25221-3 Pa. **$8.95**

SYMPHONY NO. 8 IN G MAJOR, OP. 88, SYMPHONY NO. 9 IN E MINOR, OP. 95 ("NEW WORLD") IN FULL SCORE, Antonín Dvořák. Two celebrated symphonies by the great Czech composer, the Eighth and the immensely popular Ninth, "From the New World" in one volume. 272pp. 9 × 12.

24749-X Pa. **$13.95**

FOUR ORCHESTRAL WORKS IN FULL SCORE: Rapsodie Espagnole, Mother Goose Suite, Valses Nobles et Sentimentales, and Pavane for a Dead Princess, Maurice Ravel. Four of Ravel's most popular orchestral works, reprinted from original full-score French editions. 240pp. 9⅜ × 12¼. (Not available in France or Germany)

25962-5 Pa. **$12.95**

COMPLETE CONCERTI GROSSI IN FULL SCORE, Arcangelo Corelli. All 12 concerti in the famous late nineteenth-century edition prepared by violinist Joseph Joachim and musicologist Friedrich Chrysander. 240pp. 8⅜ × 11¼. 25606-5 Pa. **$12.95**

PIANO CONCERTOS NOS. 11–16 IN FULL SCORE, Wolfgang Amadeus Mozart. Authoritative Breitkopf & Härtel edition of six staples of the concerto repertoire, including Mozart's cadenzas for Nos. 12–16. 256pp. 9⅜ × 12¼. 25468-2 Pa. **$12.95**

NUTCRACKER SUITE IN FULL SCORE, Peter Ilyitch Tchaikovsky. Among the most popular ballet pieces ever created—a complete, inexpensive, high-quality score to study and enjoy. 128pp. 9 × 12. 25379-1 Pa. **$8.95**

TONE POEMS, SERIES I: DON JUAN, TOD UND VERKLARUNG, and DON QUIXOTE, Richard Strauss. Three of the most often performed and recorded works in entire orchestral repertoire, reproduced in full score from original editions. Study score. 286pp. 9⅜ × 12¼. (Available in U.S. only) 23754-0 Pa. **$13.95**

TONE POEMS, SERIES II: TILL EULENSPIEGELS LUSTIGE STREICHE, ALSO SPRACH ZARATHUSTRA, and EIN HELDENLEBEN, Richard Strauss. Three important orchestral works, including very popular *Till Eulenspiegel's Merry Pranks,* reproduced in full score from original editions. Study score. 315pp. 9⅜ × 12¼. (Available in U.S. only) 23755-9 Pa. **$14.95**

DAS LIED VON DER ERDE IN FULL SCORE, Gustav Mahler. Mahler's masterpiece, a fusion of song and symphony, reprinted from the original 1912 Universal Edition. English translations of song texts. 160pp. 9 × 12. 25657-X Pa. **$9.95**

SYMPHONIES NOS. 1 AND 2 IN FULL SCORE, Gustav Mahler. Unabridged, authoritative Austrian editions of Symphony No. 1 in D Major ("Titan") and Symphony No. 2 in C Minor ("Resurrection"). 384pp. 8⅛ × 11. 25473-9 Pa. **$14.95**

SYMPHONIES NOS. 3 AND 4 IN FULL SCORE, Gustav Mahler. Two brilliantly contrasting masterworks—one scored for a massive ensemble, the other for small orchestra and soloist—reprinted from authoritative Viennese editions. 368pp. 9⅜ × 12¼. 26166-2 Pa. **$16.95**

SYMPHONY NO. 8 IN FULL SCORE, Gustav Mahler. Superb authoritative edition of massive, complex "Symphony of a Thousand." Scored for orchestra, eight solo voices, double chorus, boys' choir and organ. Reprint of Izdatel'stvo "Muzyka," Moscow, edition. Translation of texts. 272pp. 9⅜ × 12¼. 26022-4 Pa. **$12.95**

GREAT ROMANTIC VIOLIN CONCERTI IN FULL SCORE, Ludwig van Beethoven, Felix Mendelssohn and Peter Ilyitch Tchaikovsky. The Beethoven Op. 61, Mendelssohn, Op. 64 and Tchaikovsky, Op. 35 concertos reprinted from the Breitkopf & Härtel editions. 224pp. 9 × 12.
24989-1 Pa. **$10.95**

MAJOR ORCHESTRAL WORKS IN FULL SCORE, Felix Mendelssohn. Generally considered to be Mendelssohn's finest orchestral works, here in one volume are: the complete *Midsummer Night's Dream; Hebrides Overture; Calm Sea and Prosperous Voyage Overture;* Symphony No. 3 in A ("Scottish"); and Symphony No. 4 in A ("Italian"). Breitkopf & Härtel edition. Study score. 406pp. 9 × 12.
23184-4 Pa. **$18.95**

COMPLETE SYMPHONIES, Johannes Brahms. Full orchestral scores. No. 1 in C Minor, Op. 68; No. 2 in D Major, Op. 73; No. 3 in F Major, Op. 90; and No. 4 in E Minor, Op. 98. Reproduced from definitive Vienna Gesellschaft der Musikfreunde edition. Study score. 344pp. 9 × 12.
23053-8 Pa. **$14.95**

THE VIOLIN CONCERTI AND THE SINFONIA CONCERTANTE, K.364, IN FULL SCORE, Wolfgang Amadeus Mozart. All five violin concerti and famed double concerto reproduced from authoritative Breitkopf & Härtel Complete Works Edition. 208pp. 9⅜ × 12½.
25169-1 Pa. **$12.95**

17 DIVERTIMENTI FOR VARIOUS INSTRUMENTS, Wolfgang A. Mozart. Sparkling pieces of great vitality and brilliance from 1771–1779; consecutively numbered from 1 to 17. Reproduced from definitive Breitkopf & Härtel Complete Works edition. Study score. 241pp. 9⅜ × 12¼.
23862-8 Pa. **$13.95**

WATER MUSIC AND MUSIC FOR THE ROYAL FIREWORKS IN FULL SCORE, George Frideric Handel. Full scores of two of the most popular Baroque orchestral works performed today—reprinted from definitive Deutsche Handelgesellschaft edition. Total of 96pp. 8⅜ × 11.
25070-9 Pa. **$7.95**

FOURTH, FIFTH AND SIXTH SYMPHONIES IN FULL SCORE, Peter Ilyitch Tchaikovsky. Complete orchestral scores of Symphony No. 4 in F minor, Op. 36; Symphony No. 5 in E minor, Op. 64; Symphony No. 6 in B minor, "Pathetique," Op. 74. Study score. Breitkopf & Härtel editions. 480pp. 9⅜ × 12¼.   23861-X Pa. **$19.95**

ROMEO AND JULIET OVERTURE AND CAPRICCIO ITALIEN IN FULL SCORE, Peter Ilyitch Tchaikovsky. Two of Russian master's most popular compositions in high quality, inexpensive reproduction. From authoritative Russian edition. 208pp. 8⅜ × 11½.
25217-5 Pa. **$10.95**

DAPHNIS AND CHLOE IN FULL SCORE, Maurice Ravel. Definitive full-score edition of Ravel's rich musical setting of a Greek fable by Longus is reprinted here from the original French edition. 320pp. 9⅜ × 12¼. (Not available in France or Germany) 25826-2 Pa. **$15.95**

THREE GREAT ORCHESTRAL WORKS IN FULL SCORE, Claude Debussy. Three favorites by influential modernist: *Prélude à l'Après-midi d'un Faune, Nocturnes,* and *La Mer.* Reprinted from early French editions. 279pp. 9 × 12. 24441-5 Pa. **$13.95**

SYMPHONY IN D MINOR IN FULL SCORE, César Franck. Superb, authoritative edition of Franck's only symphony, an often-performed and recorded masterwork of late French romantic style. 160pp. 9 × 12. 25373-2 Pa. **$9.95**

THE GREAT WALTZES IN FULL SCORE, Johann Strauss, Jr. Complete scores of eight melodic masterpieces: The Beautiful Blue Danube, Emperor Waltz, Tales of the Vienna Woods, Wiener Blut, four more. Authoritative editions. 336pp. 8⅜ × 11¼. 26009-7 Pa. **$14.95**

THE FIREBIRD IN FULL SCORE (Original 1910 Version), Igor Stravinsky. Handsome, inexpensive edition of modern masterpiece, renowned for brilliant orchestration, glowing color. Authoritative Russian edition. 176pp. 9⅜ × 12¼. (Available in U.S. only) 25535-2 Pa. **$10.95**

PETRUSHKA IN FULL SCORE: Original Version, Igor Stravinsky. The definitive full-score edition of Stravinsky's masterful score for the great Ballets Russes 1911 production of *Petrushka.* 160pp. 9⅜ × 12¼. (Available in U.S. only) 25680-4 Pa. **$9.95**

MAJOR ORCHESTRAL WORKS IN FULL SCORE, Felix Mendelssohn. Generally considered to be Mendelssohn's finest orchestral works, here in one volume are: the complete *Midsummer Night's Dream; Hebrides Overture; Calm Sea and Prosperous Voyage Overture;* Symphony No. 3 in A ("Scottish"); and Symphony No. 4 in A ("Italian"). Breitkopf & Härtel edition. Study score. 406pp. 9 × 12. 23184-4 Pa. **$18.95**

DOVER MINIATURE SCORES

Bach, J. S. THE SIX BRANDENBURG CONCERTOS, BWV 1046–1051. (29795-0) $4.95

Beethoven, Ludwig van. LATE STRING QUARTETS AND THE GROSSE FUGE, OPP. 127, 130–133, 135. (40111-1) $4.95

Beethoven, Ludwig van. SYMPHONY NO. 3 IN E-FLAT MAJOR, OP. 55 ("EROICA"). (29796-9) $2.95

Beethoven, Ludwig van. SYMPHONY NO. 5 IN C MINOR, OP. 67. (29850-7) $2.95

Beethoven, Ludwig van. SYMPHONY NO. 6 IN F MAJOR, OP. 68 ("PASTORALE"). (40123-5) $2.95

Beethoven, Ludwig van. SYMPHONY NO. 9 IN D MINOR, OP. 125 ("CHORAL"). (29924-4) $4.95

Berlioz, Hector. SYMPHONIE FANTASTIQUE, OP. 14 (EPISODE IN THE LIFE OF AN ARTIST). (29890-6) $4.95

Brahms, Johannes. SYMPHONY NO. 1 IN C MINOR, OP. 68. (29797-7) $2.95

Brahms, Johannes. SYMPHONY NO. 3 IN F MAJOR, OP. 90. (40125-1) $2.95

Brahms, Johannes. SYMPHONY NO. 4 IN E MINOR, OP. 98. (29891-4) $3.95

Debussy, Claude. LA MER (THE SEA): THREE SYMPHONIC SKETCHES. (29848-5) $3.95

Dvořák, Antonín. SYMPHONY NO. 9 IN E MINOR, OP. 95 ("FROM THE NEW WORLD"). (29892-2) $2.95

Haydn, Joseph. SYMPHONY NO. 104 IN D MAJOR ("LONDON"). (29925-2) $2.95

Mahler, Gustav. SYMPHONY NO. 2 IN C MINOR ("RESURRECTION"). (29952-X) $4.95

Mahler, Gustav. SYMPHONY NO. 5 IN C-SHARP MINOR. (40115-4) $4.95

Mendelssohn, Felix. SYMPHONY NO. 4 IN A MAJOR, OP. 90 ("ITALIAN"). (29953-8) $2.95

Mozart, Wolfgang A. REQUIEM, K626, IN FULL SCORE. (40116-2) $3.95

Mozart, Wolfgang A. SYMPHONY NO. 40 IN G MINOR, K550, AND SYMPHONY NO. 41 IN C MAJOR, K551 ("JUPITER"). (29849-3) $3.95

Schubert, Franz. SYMPHONY NO. 8 IN B MINOR, D759 ("UNFINISHED"), AND SYMPHONY NO. 9 IN C MAJOR, D944 ("THE GREAT"). (29923-6) $3.95

Tchaikovsky, Peter. SYMPHONY NO. 5 IN E MINOR, OP. 64. (40133-2) $4.95

Tchaikovsky, Peter. SYMPHONY NO. 6 IN B MINOR, OP. 74 ("PATHÉTIQUE"). (29954-6) $4.95

Free Dover Music Scores and Books Catalog (59057-7) available upon request.

LUDWIG VAN BEETHOVEN

SYMPHONY NO. 6
in F Major, Op. 68
"Pastorale"

During his favorite rambles through the countryside, Beethoven sought inspiration in his natural surroundings. His Symphony No. 6, the "Pastorale," particularly reflects the composer's deep love of nature. Reproduced here from the authoritative H. Litolff edition, the work has long been a staple of the orchestral repertoire.

Each of the symphony's five movements bears a programmatic inscription. The slow movement, for example, labelled "Scene by the brook," delights with its stylized birdcalls—courtesy of the woodwinds—featuring the quail, nightingale, and cuckoo. Overall, however, the music is less about depicting specific scenes and more about evoking the emotions aroused by the natural world.

The work appears here in full score, with bar-numbered movements and ample margins at the bottom of each score page for notes and analysis. Ideal for study in the classroom, at home, or in the concert hall, this affordable, high-quality, conveniently sized volume will be the edition of choice for music students and music lovers alike.

Unabridged Dover (1998) republication of the H. Litolff edition. Contents. Instrumentation. 96 pp. 5¾ x 8. Paperbound.

Free Dover Complete Music Catalog (59057-7) available upon request.

ISBN 0-486-40123

$2.95 IN USA

9 780486 401232

THE
PSYCHIC
SOURCEBOOK

HOW TO CHOOSE
AND USE A PSYCHIC

A comprehensive consumer guide to
• Card Readers • Clairvoyants • Astrologers • Healers
• Channelers • And other New Age consultants

FREDERICK G. LEVINE

 WARNER BOOKS 38729-0 $9.95 U.S.A. (38730-4 $13.50 CAN.)